TRUE BELIEVERS
OR
SYNTHETIC SAINTS

SAMUEL GORDON

TRUE BELIEVERS OR SYNTHETIC SAINTS
Copyright © 1990 by Samuel Gordon

Printed And Published By
AMBASSADOR PRODUCTIONS LTD.
Providence House
16 Hillview Avenue
Belfast BT5 6JR

37 Leconfield Road,
Loughborough,
Leics. LE11 3SP

ISBN 0 907927 58 0

CONTENTS

DEDICATION

To my pastor - Cliff Bailey

"Your love has given me great
joy and encouragement, because
you, brother, have refreshed
the hearts of the saints"
(Philemon vs.7)

FOREWORD

Here is another choice contribution from the pen of the Rev. Samuel Gordon on a marvellous portion of Scripture.

Jude's letter has a most timely message for Christians and the church in the 1990's as it probes and exposes our half-heartedness, spiritual lethargy and apostasy. Yet, at the same time, it reminds us of our enormous privileges as children and servants of the living God; of His judgement but also of God's eternal grace, mercy and peace. Interlaced through the text are fascinating references to individuals and incidents in Old Testament times and history.

But why read *this* commentary? Sam Gordon, in plain terms, has a remarkable gift for making the profound splendidly simple (preachers, please take note!). Issues of authorship, background and the like are handled in a deft way that would interest and intrigue all but the most reluctant reader. Pervading the book is an affectionate and persuasive directness, as though the author is at your very elbow. He writes the truth in crisp, pithy sentences, illuminates it by telling similes and conveys it to mind and heart in a contemporary language which sparkles with life but never descends to the cheap and irreverent.

Take up Jude's letter; read it. As you do so, open these pages. Meditate on both (Selah!). This slim volume will not take you away from Scripture but magnify and distil the message that it contains. You will be taught, enriched, humbled and mightily encouraged.

What of the author himself? He is no armchair academic and writer but a man with a pastor's heart and experience. He has been through deep personal pain and suffering, yet is throbbing with passion and desire for the kingdom of God and the glory of Christ through his present itinerant ministry.

It is, therefore, with great pleasure that I commend this book to the reading Christian public.

John M. V. Blanshard

John M. V. Blanshard
Sutton Bonington

John Blanshard is currently vice-president of the Faith Mission and vice-chairman of the U.C.C.F. He is an elder in his local fellowship in Leicestershire. In professional life he is Professor of Food Science at Nottingham University.

INTRODUCTION

'BE ALERT! The world needs all the lerts it can get.'

So declares the famous cliche. It is a well-worn sentiment in many circles. Oh yes, it is something we naturally chuckle at. But the more we think about it the more we realise how true it really is.

That's primarily what this book is all about. It is a call to arms. It is a stirring challenge to contend for the Faith. With the darkness deepening by the hour we need to be vigilant. In the trenches, on the frontline, we are called to battle.

Wide awake we view the enemy advancing. We see many foundations crumbling. So much in our society is falling apart at the seams.

Satan is on the warpath and his is a militant ministry of disintegration and deception. He is not only unleashing his ferocious attacks from the outside. That is bad enough. No, he is operating successfully on the inside. It is the enemy within! He has infiltrated our ranks. Therein lies the enormous danger.

That is why we need to be on red alert. To be on constant guard should be the aim and objective of every real believer.

I'm not guilty of being an alarmist. But I make no apology for sounding an alarm! I confess to being a realist in the midst of a topsy-turvy world.

Come with me. Take the blinkers off. Hear what Jude has to say. Draw your own conclusions. And, wherever you are, BE ALERT!

P.S.   'Selah' means *'stop and think'*.

1

LAST BUT ONE

And so it is. You know what I mean, don't you. The book of Jude is the penultimate one in the library of the word of God. It comes immediately before the Revelation and proceeds directly after 3 John.

It is only a single chapter occupying not more than a couple of pages in the average size Bible. It comprises 25 verses in total and can be read within minutes.

To be number 65 out of a possible 66 in the canon of scripture means that so often his pertinent and straight from the shoulder message is skipped over. His veracious message is often bypassed by those who immerse themselves in the mystique of the Revelation. Perhaps they are looking for something more grandiose and sensational as they seek to unravel the mysteries of the Apocalypse. To put it mildly, that is a terrible shame and great pity.

He may be little. But, he has a lot to say. He is not given to verbosity. But every word counts. He knows where he is going. And, he gets there.

Unfortunately, his book is one of the more neglected portions. Can you honestly remember the last time you listened to a sermon preached on Jude? When was the last occasion your daily reading manual touched upon Jude? Have you ever picked up another commentary on Jude as you have browsed through the well-laden shelves of your favourite christian bookshop? The chances are that the answers to all three questions are negative.

Assuming that is the case, permit me to introduce you to the man and his message. On the other hand, if you have met him before, don't give in to the temptation to flick over a few pages. Hold fire. This will be an ideal refresher course tailormade for you!

When did he write it?

I wish I knew! It's like Heinz - there are 57 answers to the six million dollar question. No-one knows. We can only assume and presume as we tentatively read between the lines. In one sense, we are groping in the dark. Yet, there are shafts of light beaming through.

It was obviously penned during the rapid rise of gnosticism. That much is clear from the inferences in the book itself. Another factor to take into consideration is that the Faith was slowly but surely being corrupted by impostors. The words of warning from the apostles have had ample time to do the rounds and are now proving to be true. The fact that Jude refers to what the apostles said rather than wrote would seem to suggest that we are still moving within the oral period. Those were the days when apostolic teaching was passed on by word of mouth.

Drawing the various strands together it would lend itself to the view that he put quill to parchment during the early years of the second half of the first century.

How was it accepted?

It is really quite incredible but the vast majority of the early church fathers had little or no difficulty in recognising the authenticity of Jude's epistle. It finds a place in the second century Muratorian canon. Tertullian viewed it as an authoritative christian document. So did Clement of Alexandria who actually wrote a commentary on it. Origen hints there were doubts in his day, but clearly he did not share them, for he said: "Jude wrote an epistle, tiny in the extreme, but yet full of powerful words and heavenly grace."

But that is not all. Athenagoras, Polycarp and Barnabas seem to have cited the epistle early in the second century. Jerome also acknowledged it as a genuine article. By the time the year 200 A.D. had dawned it was freely accepted in the main areas of the ancient church, i.e. Alexandria, Rome and Africa, as being a Spirit inspired piece of literature whose human author was Jude.

Who is he writing to?

Again, like the dating of the letter, we have no clear indication as to the recipients of his timely note. We do not know whether they were specifically of Gentile origin or Jewish extraction. Their exact and precise geographical location is also shrouded in mystery (cf. verses 3 - 5).

He himself is a Jew and that colours his thinking and taints his theology. He assumes their knowledge of inter-testamental and apocryphal literature. He takes if for granted that they are familiar with what was written during the 400 silent years between Malachi and Matthew. Over and over again he makes reference to happenings recorded in the pages of the Old Testament (cf. verse 11).

One writer hits the nail on the head when he concludes: "The references are such that only a Jew could understand them, and its allusions are such that only a Jew could catch them." He is probably right!

What makes this book different?

Well, within the confines of the New Testament he is quite unique. He quotes freely and fully from Jewish apocryphal literature. Let me give you same examples:

The information in verse 9 is gleaned from the Assumption of Moses whereas the gist of what is enshrined in verses 14 and 15 is documented from the book of Enoch. He may also have been referring to the Testament of Naphtali in verse 6 and to the Testament of Asher in verse 8.

Now there is nothing wrong with that! A high view of the

11

doctrine of biblical inspiration does not preclude the writer's privilege to quote at random from outside sources.

He can find an ally in the apostle Paul who selected relevant data from extra-biblical Jewish writings in 1 Corinthians 10:7 and 2 Timothy 3:8. He even culled some illustrative material from the heathen poets in his famous and memorable sermon at Athens (cf. Acts 17:28) and in his pastoral letter to Titus (cf. Titus 1:12). So, Jude is in respected and esteemed company!

What we have before us, therefore, is the very word of God. As such, it demands our obedience and deserves our whole-hearted allegiance. And, never more so, in the light of the times in which we live!

Selah ...

Chapter one may have appeared rather technical as we sketched the background to the book. Hopefully, you are now consciously aware and amazed at where it fits in God's unfolding agenda.

Jude was the right man for the job. But, that's how God works even in our generation. Humanly speaking, it may appear coincidental - but nothing happens by chance when God is in it!

2

RAISON D'ETRE

The question going through the mind of Mr. and Mrs. Average is: *why did Jude write his letter in the first place?* That poser is both obvious and inevitable and one that deserves a straight answer. No ground is gained by being evasive. How can we justify Jude's comments?

He is, as it were, making a contrast between truth and error. He is establishing clear lines of demarcation between the real and the spurious. He is focussing attention on the glaring difference between those who are genuine and those who are synthetic. People in the latter mould have an artificial faith which will neither stand the test of time or eternity. Having forsaken that which is true, they have embraced that which is false.

Apostasy is the name of the game they are playing. They are in the purest sense of the word: apostates! His letter shows they were making their presence felt in many local assemblies of God's people. They were dressed up in another gospel garb as they infiltrated one church after another. They claimed to be someone or something which they were not. Impostors!

Their 'christianity' is theoretical not experiential. It is all in the mind and has never touched or transformed the heart. They know the truth from A to Z but neither live by it or act upon it.

They are phony preachers and bogus believers! They are cosmetic christians! That adds a new dimension to the phrase. The word *'cosmetic'* comes from the Greek word *'kosmetikos'* which means a *'decorating or covering over'*. It is to dress up something to give it an appearance on the surface that it lacks in reality. Their religion is skin-deep. It is superficial.

An apostate is someone who has received a measure of light but not life. He may have partaken, in some degree, of the written word; but he has not welcomed the living word into his life.

A superb illustration of this is found in the well-known parable of the sower. Brilliant light is thereby cast on the shadowy life of an apostate. In that story our Lord revealed that there is a class of men, likened to seed sown on rocky ground, who *"receive the word with joy when they hear it, but they have no root. They believe for a while, but in time of testing they fall away"* (cf. Luke 8:13). The phrase *'fall away'* chosen by Luke is actually the verb form of *'apostasy'*.

An apostate is therefore one who receives the word, believes it for a time, then drifts away. How can this be? Well, one possible explanation lies in the careful choice of language used by the Spirit of God in the compiling of the accounts of this parable in the synoptic gospels. Although stony ground hearers are said to *'receive'* the word (*'dekomai'*), a much stronger term in the Greek is used of the good ground hearers. It is *'paradekomai'* as recorded in Mark 4:20. In direct contrast with the others, the good ground group *'receives to the side'* the word of the Lord by welcoming it gladly into their hearts.

Those who *'fall away'* are not said to understand the word nor do they bring forth fruit (cf. Matthew 13:23). Ironically, they don't even have roots! This analogy Jude later draws upon in verse 12 when he says apostates are *"without fruit and uprooted - twice dead."*

There is no point in us shrugging our shoulders and saying 'that was then.' It is not a phenomenon restricted and con-

14

fined to the past. It was not a seven day wonder in the first century of the primitive christian movement. No, no, a thousand times 'no.' It is bang up to date. The word of Jude is a clarion call to the slumbering church of the twentieth century to rouse herself. We need to wake up. Having wiped the sleep from our eyes we need to get up, and do something positive about it!

Satan is on the loose. He is on the run. He knows his days are numbered and his time is short. As an angel of light his strategy in these last days is to attack the church from within. Given time he will do all in his power to rob the church of her life and heart.

There are many organisations and denominations that litter the highway who once were pulsating with life. Today they are dead or dying! They were vibrant! Now their bones rattle and vibrate on the graveyard of christendom.

What has brought about the radical change in their fortunes? Generally speaking, they didn't buckle under pressure from outside. It was not the heel of external oppression and opposition that caused them to crumble and crash. No, it came from within! It was the internal and infernal foe!

Jude's timely letter is a warning to beware. We see what makes a real believer tick. But, we also discover how a synthetic saint goes about his business of undermining the work of God.

Selah ...

Jude was a brave man! He didn't cower in a corner. No, he stood his ground and bared his heart. He wore his religion on his sleeve as a man of steely conviction. That is what it takes if we are to expose error and firmly stand for truth!

3

A SPRINGBOARD TO STUDY

That is the noble and principal aim of this chapter. It is to open up the text in such a way that budding preachers will see where they are going and ultimately achieve their goal. An outline is invaluable if we are to get the most out of any section of the word. Follow it through for yourself. If you like it, feel free to use it! If you don't, then proceed to chapter 4.

verse 1a	*"Jude"*	the signature of the man
	"servant"	the spirit of the man
	"brother"	the status of the man

verse 1b	The Persons he Describes	
	"called"	it is a call to service for Christ
		it is a call to satisfaction with Christ
		it is a call to scrutiny by Christ
	"loved"	think of its majesty
		think of its measure
		think of its mystery
	"kept"	a fact to be enjoyed
		an act to be experienced

verse 2	The Prayer he Desires	
	"mercy"	that's the inflow
	"peace"	that's the downflow
	"love"	that's the overflow

verse 3

    (a)   A Word of Endearment
            "dear friends"

    (b)   Some words of Enrichment
            re. his method: *"write to you"*
            re. his manner: *"was very eager"*
            re. his message: *"salvation we share"*

    (c)   A few words of Explanation
            his sensitivity: *"I felt I had to"*
            his suitability: *"write and urge"*

    (d)   More words of Encouragement
            Faith's content: *"the Faith"*
            Faith's custodians: *"entrusted to saints"*
            Faith's completeness: *"once for all "*
            Faith's contenders: *"contend for the Faith"*

verse 4

    (a)   their Deceit
            "secretly slipped in among you"

    (b)   their Designation
            "whose condemnation was written about"

    (c)   their Description
            "they are godless men"

    (d)   their Deeds
            *"who change the grace of our God into a
            licence for immorality"*

    (e)   their Denial
            of *"Jesus Christ our only Sovereign and Lord"*
            as Monarch
            as Master
            as Mediator
            as Messiah

verses 5/6

    (a)   Something to be Remembered
            their forgetfulness: *"I want to remind you"*
            their familiarity: *"though you already know
                            all this"*

(b) Something to be Realised

a Person:	*"the Lord"*
a people:	*"His people"*
a place:	*"Egypt"*
a power:	*"delivered His people out of"*
a problem:	*"who did not believe"*
a principle:	*"later destroyed those"*

(c) Something to be Recognised

their activity: *"angels who did not keep their positions"*

their abandonment: *"abandoned their own home"*

their abode: *"kept in darkness, bound with everlasting chains"*

their appointment: *"for judgement on the great Day"*

verse 7

(a) The Pattern that has Emerged
i. wickedness of the most powerful kind in v.5
ii. wickedness of the most perverted kind in v.6
iii. wickedness of the most polluted kind in v.7

(b) The Places that are Enlisted
"Sodom and Gomorrah and the surrounding towns"

(c) The Practices that are Exposed
they *"gave themselves up to sexual immorality and perversion"*

(d) The Punishment that was Effected
"they serve as an example of those who suffer the punishment of eternal fire"

(e) The Parallels that are Evident
TODAY: the endemic of AIDS from the GAY lifestyle

19

          (f) The Power that can be Experienced
              cf. 1 Corinthians 6:9-11 *"such were some of you"*

verse 8   They dream: *"these dreamers"*
                They defile: *"pollute their own bodies"*
                They despise: *"reject authority"*
                They decry: *"slander celestial beings"*

verse 9   The meaning: *"Michael"*
                The manager: *"the archangel"*
                The ministry: *"disputing with the devil"*
                The method: *"did not dare to bring a slanderous accusation against him"*
                The message: *"the Lord rebuke you"*

verse 10

        (a)   The Subject of their Conversation
              "whatever they do not understand"

        (b)   The Slant in their Communication
              "they speak abusively"

        (c)   The Sphere of their Corruption
              "and what things they do understand by instinct, like unreasoning animals - these are the very things that destroy them"

verse 11

        (a)   A solemn pronouncement
              "woe to them"

        (b)   A suggested progression
              the tragedy in our text
              the trend in our text
              the thought in our text

(c)   A serious presentation

"way of Cain"   - rebellion against the way to
                               God

"Balaam's error"   - rebellion against the walk with
                               God

"Korah's rebellion" - rebellion against the worship
                               of God

verses 12/13

(a)   The selection of the similes

(b)   The suggestiveness of the similes
"blemishes at your love feasts"
"clouds without rain"
"autumn trees"
"wild waves of the sea"
"wandering stars"

(c)   The synopsis of the similes
seen when taken together (cf. verses 5-7)

(d)   The significance of the similes
seen in the contrast between the real
believer and the synthetic saint

verse 14a

His birth:	*"the seventh from Adam"*
His world:	cf. Genesis 6:5
His son:	Methuselah
His faith:	was fixed in Jehovah
His walk:	for 300 years with God
His translation:	he never died!
His future:	possible mention in Revelation 11

21

verses 14b/15

    (a)   A blessed sentiment
    "see"
    "the Lord is coming"
    "with thousands upon thousands of his holy ones"

    (b)   A bold statement
    "to judge everyone, and to convict all the ungodly of all the ungodly acts they have done in the ungodly way, and of all the harsh words ungodly sinners have spoken against him"

verse 16

    Their Grumbling Attitude: *"grumblers"*
    Their Glib Accusations: *"fault-finders"*
    Their Grotesque Activity: *"they follow their own evil desires"*
    Their Gross Arrogance: *"they boast about themselves"*
    Their General Ambition: *"flatter others for their own advantage"*

verses 17/18

    (a)   A need to look again
        "but" - the change that is effective
        "dear friends" - the contrast that is evident

    (b)   A need to look back
        "remember what the apostles of our Lord Jesus Christ foretold"

    (c)   A need to look around
        "apostles"   - their definition
                      - their doctrine
                      - their distinctiveness
                      - their disappearance

(d)   A need to look in
      "scoffers" - their identification
      "follow their own" - their independence
      "ungodly desires" - their innovations
      "in last times!" - their incursion
      They're doomed! - their impeachment

(e)   A need to look out
      these are the last times - it is happening
      before our very eyes

(f)   A need to look up
      for Christ is returning!

verse 19
(a)   They are sectarian in their approach
      "these are the men who divide you"

(b)   They are self-centred in their ambitions
      "who follow mere natural instincts"

(c)   They are sinners in the assembly
      "and do not have the Spirit"

verse 20a   *"But you dear friends"*
(a)   reveals the reality of their religion
(b)   describes the distinctiveness of their doctrine
(c)   denotes the depth of their duty
(d)   reflects the riches of their resources

verse 20b
(a)   Labouring in the Scriptures
      "most holy faith" - the stability that is emphasised
      "your" - the saint that is exercised
      "build yourselves up" - the study that is envisaged
When we do this - the strength that is experienced

(b)   Leaning on the Spirit
"the Holy Spirit" - an appreciation of His name
"pray" - an awareness of our need
"in the" - an assurance of His nearness

verse 21a
- (a)   The value of such a love
  "God's love"

- (b)   The validity of such logic
  "keep yourselves"

- (c)   The vantage of such a location
  "in God's love"

verse 21b
- (a)   There is everlasting life for a look at the crucified One

- (b)   There is an exchanged life for a look at the crowned One

- (c)   There is an encouraging life for a look at the compassionate One

- (d)   There is eternal life for a look at the coming One
  "as you wait for the mercy of our Lord Jesus Christ to bring you to eternal life"

verses 22/23
- (a)   Those in doubt
  "be merciful to those who doubt"

- (b)   Those in danger
  "snatch others from the fire and save them"

24

(c)   Those departed
       *"to others show mercy mixed with fear -
       hating even the clothing stained by corrupted
       flesh"*

verses 24/25

(a)   A God who is sufficient in His power
       "To Him who is able"

(b)   A God who is sovereign in His purpose
       *"to keep you from falling and to present you
       before His glorious presence without fault
       and with great joy"*

(c)   A God who is supreme in His preeminence
       "to the only God our Saviour"

(d)   A God who is superlative in His praise
       *"be glory, majesty, power and authority ...
       before all ages, now and for evermore"*

Selah ...
*Yes, it's only an outline! Nothing more than a skeleton.
Don't keep it in the cupboard of your mind. Add some flesh
to it. Make it yours. You will be surprised what can happen
both to you and your contemporaries when you personalise
these pointers for further study. Go on ... have a go ... you
have nothing to lose!*

4

WITH A NAME LIKE THAT

The first word *'Jude'* is the signature of the man. Now we know who has penned the letter. I am intrigued by his introduction. All he says is: Jude. Nothing more. Nothing else. Just Jude!

That shows me something of the humility of the man. There are no airs or graces with this man, no lofty titles or appellations. There is no indication of a *'holier than thou'* attitude being adopted. Nor is he pushy about his particular brand of christianity. He is very much down to earth. He radiates the gospel as he shines for Jesus in the midst of an inky black environment.

But, oh what a name! It seems a shame that someone so nice should be handicapped with such an unfortunate choice of name. Nevertheless, he is not responsible for what his parents inflicted upon him. Isn't it wonderful though how God takes it and uses it to speak volumes to many needy hearts?

In the original Greek this name is Judas! Ah, that rings a bell. Judas - the name has been synonymous with betrayal for years. It has been anathema since the first century when Judas engaged in an act of treachery and sold the Lord Jesus for a few silver coins. He was a traitor! He became the worst apostate the world has ever known.

Now, in the providence of God, this single word ushers in a chapter devoted to the subject of apostasy within the professing church during the last days.

The plot begins to thicken, however, when we try to sort out which Judas we are thinking about. There are no fewer than five of them mentioned on the pages of the New Testament.

Number One: he was the Judas of Damascus in whose home Paul was praying after his miraculous life changing conversion to faith in Jesus. You can read about him in Acts 9:11.

Number Two: Judas Barsabas was a leading light in the councils of the early church. He, alongside Silas, conveyed the message to the church at Antioch concerning the decision of the Jerusalem council to throw open their doors to Gentiles. He was also recognised as a prophet (cf. Acts 15:22,27,32).

Number Three: There was the notorious Judas Iscariot. He was described as the *'son of perdition'* who ended his life by committing suicide.

None of these three has ever seriously been considered as likely contenders for the authorship of this punchy letter. So, we will follow the tradition of our fathers and likewise rule them out! That leaves two more candidates for our screening and vetting process.

Number Four: Within the ranks of the apostolic band, there was a second Judas. He is distinguished by John as *'Judas not Iscariot'* (cf. John 14:22). In Luke's compilation of the Twelve there is an apostle whom the record refers to as *'Judas son of James'* (cf. Luke 6:16). The two are speaking about the same individual. This therefore cancels his possible eligibility.

There is only one Judas left ... well, there had to be, didn't there. *He is number five.* The Judas who was the brother of Jesus (cf. Matthew 13:55; Mark 6:3). At the same time he could truly be called *'the brother of James'* because he was also one of our Lord's brothers. It is perfectly reasonable to assume that his conversion to faith in Christ must have taken place between the crucifixion and the ascension of his elder brother from the Mount of Olives.

And, so, by the process of elimination we have unravelled the mystery of his identification. Yes, with a name like that, most people would run a mile! But, this one is different.

He is perfectly content to see himself as *'a servant of Jesus Christ.'* He was a bondslave. He was one who was willing and eager to do whatever his master commanded. He did it out of loyalty and love.

He never used his fraternal relationship with Christ to impress other people. He was not into the deplorable habit of name dropping! Why? Jesus was not only his brother; Jesus was his Lord!

He was glad to be a servant. That was a most demanding role to play on the stage of daily life. It meant he would be second to his brother in the pecking order. James was an eminent leader in the early church and was a household name throughout the land. It would have been easy for Jude to adopt a spirit of resentment and allow a streak of jealousy to develop. That would be natural, albeit, sinful. He happily lived under the shadow of his famous brother.

That's what being a servant is all about!

Selah ...
A servant! Why stoop to be a king?

5

TWO THREES

"To those who have been called, who are loved by God the Father and kept by Jesus Christ: Mercy, peace and love be yours in abundance" (verses 1,2)

The trained eye will have already detected a double trio in the above verses. Jude is like every good preacher - he has a three point outline!

In stark contrast to the spiritual masqueraders the true christian has a wonderful relationship both with heaven and earth. The trinity has a vital role to play in the unfolding drama of salvation as it affects individual believers.

We are called by the Spirit, loved by the Father, and kept by Jesus Christ. These blessings, and countless more, are ours by virtue of our faith in a finished work wrought upon Calvary.

The word *'called'* means *'an official summons.'* That general call is issued with the proclamation of the glorious gospel. It becomes effectual when we positively respond to it. At that moment we are born and brought into the family of God. We have been summoned by Him because our salvation begins with Him doing a deep work of grace in our hearts.

To be *'loved by God the Father'* is something better felt than telt! This takes us into the realm of the sublime. It brings us not only to the threshold of His beneficience but tenderly envelops us in His heart. He loves us dearly. He loves us deeply. We are exceptionally precious to Him. It matters to Him about you and me. The same love He has shown to Jesus, His one and only Son, He showers upon us. We don't deserve it - but that's love!

To be *'kept by Jesus Christ'* means our security and safety are His complete concern. He is watching over us. He is guarding our every footstep. In the original language the word is in the present tense. That means we are continually kept. It is an ongoing ministry on our behalf. We have the grip of God upon our lives.

Our position is quite unique. We are called by God to be set apart for God so that we might enjoy love with God. That is something the apostate knows little or nothing about!

Not only does Jude show us who we are but he goes on to remind us what we have already. And, it is his yearning that we may have it in abundance. He prays that these benefits may be multiplied towards us. These will help us to cope in the coming hour of crisis when apostasy seems to be making an inroads into our assemblies.

'Mercy' underlines our relationship with God. It is an upward look. From the wealth of His mercy He freely forgives our sin. The old divines spoke of it as the *'darling attribute of deity.'* His mercy is new to us every morning as we enjoy communion with Him. In His mercy He does not give us what we deserve. Rather, He meets our every need!

'Peace' is an inward expression and highlights our relationship with ourselves. It is that inner tranquility in the midst of life's storms. It is the calm that floods our minds when anxiety is nailed to the cross. It is a deep seated contentment knowing that all is well because He is in control.

'Love' reaches out into the community where we live. It is the natural by-product of a man who had known mercy and who is at peace with himself and God. This should be the hallmark of our churches as we think of the other person's highest good.

These pedlars of error whom Jude is warning of have no real testimony of God's dealings in their lives. For them life is a soap-box opera. They are merchandisers of falsehood as they live a lie themselves. In comparison to the true christian they are mere counterfeit. As common religious criminals they seek to detract from the glory of His name.

They profess! Alas, they do not possess!

Selah ...

We have a wonderful Saviour. We have a marvellous salvation. And it gets better with every passing hour. Because, our hearts are full to the brim since mercy is the inflow, peace is the downflow, and love is the overflow!

6

A CHANGE OF MIND

"Dear friends, although I was very eager to write to you about the salvation we share, I felt I had to write and urge you to contend for the Faith that was once for all entrusted to the saints" (verse 3)

Believe it or not, he's a man in a million! He changed his mind!

He switches topic midstream in his letter. Originally the burden on his heart was to talk about their *'common salvation.'* That was something they shared together in the family of God. I wonder how he would have developed that particular theme. We can only surmise and speculate for the time being. Perhaps when we meet in eternity he will be able to answer all our queries.

He refers to his unseen audience as *'dear friends.'* Paul also followed a similar pattern in many of his epistles. The Greek word *'agapetos'* conveys the idea of a shepherd caring for his sheep who were in danger of straying; the concern of an elder for the souls of those who were in danger of slipping; the compassion of a pastor for the welfare of those who were in danger of stumbling.

That's why he *'felt he had to write'* in the manner he did. He was a man whose ear was attuned to the voice of God and his mind was attentive to the purpose of God. There was an inner compulsion, an internal force overwhelmed him. He was a man operating under pressure from the Holy Spirit.

In writing he succinctly urges them to defend the Faith that some are denying; to preserve the Faith that some are perverting; and to contend for the Faith that some are corrupting.

There is a distinction made in the New Testament between *'faith'* and *'the Faith'*. *'Faith'* refers to the act of believing; *'the Faith'* speaks of the thing believed. It is the sum total of revealed truth; the final and full revelation of God as we have it in the scriptures. It is that body of doctrine unfolded from Genesis to Revelation. The Faith is the word of God.

This has been graciously entrusted to us. We are custodians of the Faith. It was not imparted to human institutions, societies or organisations, but to the people of God. We have in our care the oracles of God. We are to be guardians of holy writ.

The mandate was delivered to us not once upon a time but *'once for all'* time. There can be no addition or subtraction. It is a finished work. A striking phrase this proves to be. The same word is used in Hebrews 9:26-28 where reference is made to the absolute finality of the atonement of Christ. Thank God, that work is complete also.

As there is no more sacrifice needed for sin, so there is no more scripture needed for the saint!

Our solemn obligation and duty today is to defend it. We must stand for the truth, with the truth, and by the truth.

In contending we must guard against being contentious. We must be careful not to bring discredit to the cause of Christ, disgrace to the character of Christ, or dishonour to the church of Christ.

As in a relay race, the baton has been passed to us. We must hand it on to the generation following close on our heels.

It is a most worthy cause as we unashamedly nail our colours to the mast. We are soldiers in the Lord's army. We should be fighting a good fight for the Faith in these days of spiritual decline.

Selah ...
The church is always one generation short of extinction. If our generation fails to guard the truth and entrust it to our children, then that will be the end!

7

KNOW YOUR ENEMY

"For certain men whose condemnation was written about long ago have secretly slipped in among you. They are godless men, who change the grace of our God into a licence for immorality and deny Jesus Christ our only Sovereign and Lord" (verse 4)

These words vividly remind us that the early church had many life-size problems. They had not attained perfection. No, they were often beset by serious difficulties.

The dilemma these *'certain men'* caused was designed to wreck spiritual fellowships. They brought in their wake a spirit of dissension and division. The infernal, internal foe was doing more untold damage than the persistent attacks from the enemy outside. There was a canker eating away at the very heart of the church. But how?

There were those among the gatherings of the Lord's people who had infiltrated the ranks. They were intruders. They were active members of Satan's securitate.

They had won over the support of a few with their extrovert personalities and an overdose of charisma. People were conned by the impressive display of these men who were slick and charmingly persuasive in their pep talk.

They had entered in the disguise of being disciples. They were hiding under the cloak of christianity. They had joined the church under false pretenses. They looked alright on the outside. But, you cannot judge a man by his mantle.

Jude says they *'secretly slipped in among'* them. They had come in through the back door. The word is used to speak of someone who has slipped furtively back into the country from which he has been expelled.

It also paints the picture of an alligator, lying on the bank of a river, and then slithering into the water so subtly, secretly, and silently that he is unnoticed.

This was their manner and means of entry. It says a lot about them, doesn't it.

Jude pulls no punches as he appropriately describes them as *'godless'* men. They are without God. On the surface they may appear the kind of people you could do business with. The outward veneer is pleasing to the eye but the heart is quite another matter. It is as black as coal.

They are *'into'* religion and have all the latest gimmicks, they know the choruses, they talk the language, they have the proper handshake and even embrace with the hallelujah hug, but there is nothing in the heart to win the admiration and praise of an all-seeing God. He sees through them!

There is an absence of moral restraint in their behaviour. They abuse their liberty making it an excuse for licence. They have no sense of shame when they commit their evil deeds. They openly flaunt their sin in a spirit of arrogance. By their conduct they are denying the grace of God. They are carnal from the inside out. And, when the camouflage is gone, it shows!

Their philosophy was simple: don't do as I do, do as I say.

As synthetic saints they *'deny Jesus Christ'* and that is always the root of the problem. Their deeds are but a reflection of their doctrine. Both are lacking in reality. Because of what they believed (or, didn't believe, for that matter) they had no conscience about their lifestyle. They had no conviction about their pursuit of promiscuity. They reasoned it was a personal matter, thereby leaving other people and God out in the cold.

These apostates denied him as Master. They denied him as

Mediator. They denied him as Messiah. They denied him as Monarch.

What began as an absence of reverence for God and his word resulted in a determined twisting and blatant distortion of the grace of God into an excuse for sin. This culminated and climaxed in an open denial of the person of our Lord Jesus Christ. They have looped the loop to such a degree that they could easily hide behind a corkscrew.

Now we know the enemy. They are Satan's undercover agents. We need to blow their cover and put them out on the pavement to wallow in their sin. They must be exposed and excommunicated. After all is said and done the verdict of Heaven is that *'their condemnation was written about long ago.'*

Selah ...

It's not only the smooth talker offering health and wealth that we need to worry about. It's also the pin-stripe suited person who dots his i's and crosses his t's. Both may be working for another commander!

8

YESTERDAY'S APOSTATES

*"Though you already know all this, I want to remind you that
the Lord delivered his people out of Egypt, but later destroyed those who did not believe. And the angels who did not
keep their positions of authority but abandoned their own
home - these he has kept in darkness, bound with everlasting
chains for judgement on the great Day. In a similar way,
Sodom and Gomorrah and the surrounding towns gave
themselves up to sexual immorality and perversion. They
serve as an example of those who suffer the punishment of
eternal fire" (verses 5-7)*

What a sobering and salutary lesson for all of us! They had
forgotten to remember. Their memories were good - albeit
short.

Apathy was public enemy number one in the early church
in dealing with these apostates. We need to guard against it
presently lest we sit back and get used to the idea. It is
perilously easy to opt for the easy life in an attempt not to rock
the boat. We may want to maintain the status quo. Unfortunately, we may have nodded off to sleep in the comfort of our
cushioned christianity and the enemy may have gained vital
ground. That's why Jude now pulls three illustrations from
the Old Testament.

The three of them are different. And yet they are the same!
They all have one thing in common. That common denomi-
nator is: they fell! And great was their collapse. Israel lost her

43

victory. The angels lost their vocation. Sodom and Gomorrah lost its virtue.

By citing these intensely pertinent examples Jude is hoping that these believers will learn from the past and become overcomers in the future. He does not want them to founder or flounder. He hopes they will not come unstuck when they face a similar situation in their own church. They ought to know better.

The first illustration brings us face to face with the miraculous. God brought them out of the land of bondage in order to bring them into a place of freedom. Redeemed from Egypt because they sheltered under the blood of the slain passover lamb, they now faced the insurmountable hurdle of the Red Sea. And, to make matters worse the enemy were rapidly advancing to the rear, there were high hills on either side, and they were hemmed in. But, God specialises in the impossible. He opened up the way ahead and led them through.

As they walked through the sandy stretches of desert en route to the promised land they had nothing to lose. In fact, they had everything to gain. When the border was in sight at Kadesh-barnea they took cold feet. They were swamped with an air of uncertainty. Doubts nagged and their enthusiasm waned when they heard the reports of the spies sent out to reconnoitre the land. They brought back the delicious mouthwatering grapes. But, they also spoke of giants stalking the land.

When put to the vote, the majority verdict won the day. The people backed down from responding to the stirring and momentous challenge issued by Joshua and Caleb. They capitulated to their groundless fears and, therefore, were catapulted into an era of watching each other die in the dunes. The result of that epic and historic decision was that the Israelites spent the next forty years going round in circles in the wilderness.

God's grave displeasure was noticeable in how he handled the situation. Here was a people who had trusted God to bring

44

them out of Egypt but who patently failed to trust the same unchanging God to take them into the land of Canaan. Unbelief was their sin. It kept them out of the place of blessing.

The lesson comes over loud and clear. Privilege brings responsibility. When God's people sin he does not view it lightly.

The gauntlet is thrown down to the believers in the early church not to swim with the tide of error but to bravely repel the foes of darkest apostasy. Failure to do so would bring its own self-inflicted consequences.

The second illustration takes us even further back in the annals of time. We move out of the terrestrial sphere into the celestial climes and ponder the judgement of fallen angels. It is not unreasonable to assume that these angels despised their rank and wilfully rejected the divine claim on their created powers. Of their own volition these exalted beings abandoned their lofty heights of power and dignity. They chose to opt out of the purpose of God for them.

They deserted their heavenly realm in a token gesture of rebellion and paid dearly for it. They have remained for thousands of years in the nether gloom bound in chains awaiting their ultimate day of judgement. The passing of time has not lightened or lessened their eventual fate. These pits of darkness in the unseen world are depicted by Peter as being underground caverns - a subterranean region - where God has them under lock and key until the Day of accountability (cf. 2 Peter 2:4). For them, at the gates of heaven, there was a way to hell!

The third illustration deals with the townsfolk of Sodom and Gomorrah. The panoramic sweep of God's judgement here is breathtaking and mind-blowing. If the people of Jude's day had failed to grasp the significance of the previous couple of incidents this one will make their hair stand on the back of their necks. It should send the shivers down their spine.

The twin towns of Sodom and Gomorrah together with their satellite settlements are infamous for one particularly heinous sin. It is homosexuality.

God was repelled by their despicable behaviour and animal like relationships. It smelt like a foul pungent aroma in his nostrils. It was vulgar. It was vile.

Their horrid and horrible acts underlined the sheer and total depravity of man. He had sunk to the depths of base carnality. He had plummetted to the gutter of sordid seamy relationships. When verse 7 is read alongside the relevant documentary in Genesis 19 we can begin to appreciate what Paul meant when he said: *'God gave them over to a depraved mind, to do what ought not to be done.'* (cf. Romans 1:28).

Does God sit idly by while men sin with men and replace virtue with vice? No! God in his holiness was determined to avenge. And he did!

The cities of the plain fell. Fire and brimstone were rained upon these red light communities with the sole purpose of bringing about their liquidation from the face of the planet. Inside an hour, God had wiped these dens of homosexuality off the earth. They became a smouldering heap of rubble. That intervention of God in an act of righteous judgement was only a prelude to their ultimate doom in eternity. It was only the curtain-raiser to their guaranteed fate at the end of time. These sexually degenerate reprobates virtually signed their own death warrant. They consigned themselves to the condemned cell.

The lesson is clear: you can't sin and win!

Jude, in bringing these three illustrations to prominence, is hoping those who tune in to his message will be shocked and shaken to their senses.

46

If we ignore the words of Jude there is no hope for the church. This should make every true believer a dedicated soul winner and ardent and loyal defender of the Faith.

God has done it before. He may yet do it again!

Selah ...
Israel disbelieved and lost her power; the angels dis-obeyed and lost their position; Sodom and Gomorrah were defiled and lost their purity - sin is sin is sin! On the balance sheet of life it is an incalculable loss - an eternal liability.

9

AS IT WAS ... SO IT IS

"In the very same way, these dreamers pollute their own bodies, reject authority and slander celestial beings" (verse 8)

History repeats itself! That is precisely what was happening in Jude's day. And, we have gone full circle in our present generation. We are back to the days Jude graphically portrayed in the preceding verses as he begins his unequivocal statement by declaring: *'in the very same way.'*

When the curtain is drawn aside we catch a glimpse of the dominant features in their character. But, we also notice the domineering factors in their conduct. They are the best of a bad bunch. What are they guilty of?

Firstly, they are dreamers. They live in a world of make believe. They often embark on fanciful flights of imagination taking them into the clouds of sensual fantasy. Their home-spun philosophy is pie-in-the-sky as they blatantly defy all logic and reason. They show a wilful disregard for recognised moral and ethical standards. Their trips into the arena of the subconscious and into the unexplored regions of the mind cause them to act in an abnormal manner. They operate in uncharted waters. Their thought life is poisoned as they are subjected to satanic and demonic influence.

Because their mind has become a cesspool of iniquity they have no conscience about their despicable activities. Their 'inner warning voice' is seared because they are wallowing

49

in a sewer. Theirs is the religion of the gutter. Sin is a way of life to them. And, the more vulgar the better. Virtue has gone out of the window. They are held firmly in the grip of vice.

As they attempt to satisfy the appetite of the flesh they indulge in the works of the flesh. Sex, sex, and more sex is their motto. The logo emblazoned on the lapel of their lives is *eros*. Irrespective of how unnatural the physical relationship may be they plunge deeper and deeper into the bottomless pit of sin.

Their bodies and minds have become pawns in the hands of Satan. They are sold out to him. They engage in passioned displays of lewdness and the more crude the better. The night clubs of Sunset Strip and Soho would gladly welcome such clientele. Their outlook is one of free love for all.

Secondly, they despise authority. They are lawless. They are a law unto themselves. Both political and ecclesiastical authority is rejected by them. Their irrational policy is simple - rules are made and meant to be broken.

Just because a law was tabled in the word of God, or a statute written into a nation's constitution, that did not matter one iota. They were hellbent in their pursuit of carnal recklessness. They unnervingly imbibed a spirit of revolt and anarchy as they embraced warmly the concept of total freedom with no restrictions attached. It was, in reality, a concession to licence. Because of their attitude and actions they are *'antichrist'* in their hearts.

They are insubordinate as they fly in the face of law and authority.

Without doubt the setting aside of the authority of scripture is incorporated in the phrase we are presently pondering. Apostates cast to the ground the word of God and trample it under foot.

Hand in hand with the spurning of God's precepts is the call for a new social order. It is a libertarian civil rights charter. Thus the phrase supplies a key to the otherwise inexplicable fact that many apostate religious leaders are often associated with subversive organisations which seek to undermine and who frequently orchestrate attempts to overthrow governments. They pronounce their pastoral blessing on freedom fighters and those who engage in long struggles for independence based on their warped liberation theology.

The reason why these impostors reject authority is because they have no wish to permit Jesus Christ to govern in their lives. They do not want a God who rules over them. They are running in the footprints of many who call out: *'Away with Him.'*

Thirdly, theirs is a life of irreverence as they degrade dignitaries. Every time they open their mouths they slander and speak evil against the Most High. They blaspheme by lip as they engage in cynicism, ridicule and short-sighted verbal abuse. They have no respect for God's appointed leaders, nor, do they esteem God's anointed messengers.

They have swallowed hook, line and sinker the bait Satan has tempted them with. They have fallen headlong into the trap he has set and now they are his willing henchmen.

That spirit of apostasy found in Jude's day is abroad in these last days. Looking around us today I sometimes wonder if the complete fulfilment of Jude's prophecy is near. There are many synthetic saints within the walls of our churches. We need to root them out and show them the door in the light of what Jude has been saying.

Selah ...
The new morality we hear about today is nothing more than the old immorality.

10

HOW TO TREAT THE DEVIL

*"But even the archangel Michael, when he was disputing
with the devil about the body of Moses, did not dare to
bring a slanderous accusation against him, but said, 'The
Lord rebuke you'" (verse 9)*

It seems a strange verse, doesn't it. Here we have a fact not
disclosed anywhere else in scripture. It deals with the
handling of Satan by Michael. And, I'm sure there is a salient
lesson here for all of us.

The name *'Michael'* actually means *'who is like unto
God.'* In other words, the angel was a reflector of the glory
and beauty of God. He got like the company he kept!

He was the manager of the heavenly host and held a
position of supreme authority. He had scaled to the top rung
of the ladder in terms of angelic rank. He has overall
responsibility for the day-to-day administration of the angelic band. He oversees all appointments within the heavenly
realm and supervises all arrangements regarding specialised
roles (cf. the seven angels in Revelation 8). In this capacity
as the commander-in-chief he is still fully responsible to the
throne of God.

Did you notice what he is doing in verse 9? He is *'disputing with the devil'* in relation to the body of Moses.

Wherever Michael is mentioned in the compass of scripture it is generally in relation to the nation of Israel and the
Jewish people. He seems to emerge as their guardian angel.

You can read about his involvment in the realm of conflict in Daniel 10. Daniel was well into his 80's and had been greatly distressed by the vision of the seventy weeks in chapter 9. He agonised in prayer as he poured out his heart to his God. For three long weeks he waited. Gradually his strength sapped. His energy was expended. He felt so weak and helpless. He couldn't understand why no answer had been forthcoming. Why the apparent delay?

God had despatched an angelic messenger to Daniel with the answer on the first day of his ordeal. However, unknown to Daniel, this angel's journey had been hindered and his progress hampered en route. Through no fault of his he was prevented by the austere personage of the *'prince of the kingdom of Persia'* (cf. Daniel 10:13). He had to pass through Satan's territory. And, the devil was determined to stop him. For twenty-one days there was no way through the impasse. The battle raged. That is, until Michael intervened!

Here, though, in Jude's letter he is embroiled in a slightly different role. It is the sphere of controversy. The old devil is again in the picture as he makes enquiries pertaining to the body of Moses.

The only reference to the body of Moses is found in Deuteronomy 34:5,6 which leads us to believe that God alone knows where His servant is buried. The precise location of his tomb is unknown to man and angel. This time Satan is out in the dark. God had hoodwinked him. This was a no-go and no-know area for the wily devil.

It is well within the permitted bounds of possibility to intelligently suggest that if the actual burial site had been revealed to man it would have become the object of much veneration.

There is no doubt that it would have rapidly turned into some kind of shrine to be visited by the devotees of many religions. It would have become another popular venue on the merry-go-round itinerary of money spinning pilgrimages.

Michael's reaction and response says it all. He knew when to keep his mouth shut. He did not lower himself in any way nor did he get involved in a shouting match with the enemy. Even though the devil was in the wrong Michael graciously refrained from addressing personal rebuke to him. He could have attempted to vindicate himself or perhaps he could have questioned the authority and motive of Satan. But, he did neither.

He clicked his heels and bluntly said: *'The Lord rebuke you.'*

He was quite content to leave the outcome with God. Judgement is exclusively His prerogative. That is His domain. He can settle every issue. And, given time, He will.

Selah ...

Perhaps like old Daniel we need to learn the lesson that God's delays are not God's denials. The answer's on the way. And, at the end of the day, God will have the final say. The last word belongs to Him.

11

ACTING LIKE ANIMALS

"Yet these men speak abusively against whatever they do not understand; and what things they do understand by instinct, like unreasoning animals - these are the very things that destroy them" (verse 10)

Jude pulls no punches. He calls a spade - a spade! His description of these impostors is both weird and gripping. It is quite sensational for men to be labelled and libelled the way they are. They're acting like animals. In fact, sometimes they're worse.

Every well rehearsed pronouncement they make from their ivory towers is pernicious. They cannot say anything good about God or man so they indulge in a concerted propaganda campaign of evil.

Their language is *'abusive'* as they blaspheme and reproach. The amazing thing is that they are lecturing and pontificating on things *'they do not understand.'*

They are self-elected and self-appointed. They are acting in such a manner as if they knew it all. They present themselves both in public and private as being the fount of all knowledge.

Yet, in the cold light of day, they are intellectual eggheads. They haven't a clue as they rant and rave in their open-ended conversations. It is the blind leading the blind on an unscheduled ramble through the maze of ill-conceived scatter-brained thoughts of these men.

They didn't know what they were talking about. But, they knew what they were doing. That came naturally. The herd instinct rose to the surface. And, that's what they followed. They are men with four legs!

Bear in mind, these are synthetic saints Jude is talking about. These are apostates he is collaring. Their sinful acts, their vulgar vices, their gross immorality, their total disregard for any of the laws of nature made them worse than the heathen pagans round about them. With their crass behaviour they had sunk to the lowest of the low. They couldn't sink much further.

Their fate is inevitable and well catalogued. Jude says, *'these are the very things that destroy them.'* They are programmed for doom. They are themselves pressing the self-destruct button. Alright, you play with fire you'll get badly burned!

Their lust burned within them and they destroyed themselves. They burned themselves out. Sin when left to run its course will take a man to the lake of fire.

From the comments Jude has made earlier wc can deduce that sin will stain a man, then spoil a man, but ultimately it will slay a man. They are firmly held in the tentacles of the enemy and they cannot break free from his clutches. Therein lies the peril of turning your back on God.

Is it any wonder Jude says what he does?

Selah ...

The world of the apostate is a murky one. The atmosphere is eerie. That's why as real believers we must consciously guard the purity of our fellowships and keep ourselves unspotted. We can't afford to become contaminated or polluted with those who pander to the flesh in the name of religion.

12

NAMING NAMES

"Woe to them! They have taken the way of Cain; they have rushed for profit into Balaam's error; they have been destroyed in Korah's rebellion" (verse 11)

Jude doesn't beat about the bush. He doesn't claim immunity from prosecution as he launches into a most enlightening presentation of some golden oldies who were apostate in their thinking. We delve back into the distant past as Jude focusses in on a trio of characters well known for their movements and mistakes. They are thumbnail sketches collated from the dusty archives of antiquity of men who fell by the wayside.

Cain was a farmer. Balaam was a prophet. Korah was a prince. You see, apostasy is not confined to any particular class of people. Every strata of society is embraced here. It touches the common man in the street, the cleric in the pulpit, and the upper crust who stalk the corridors of power.

The men Jude is talking about have not only secured access into the local church but they have gained ascendancy. They had effectively hijacked the local leadership. Theirs was not an abortive coup. They were not the backroom boys nor were they members of the back-seat brigade. They were functioning as teachers who were actively pursuing a course that would brainwash and indoctrinate their pupils.

Heaven's attitude is clear. *'Woe to them.'* That's strong language. Powerful words. Yes, they incur the wrath of God upon their souls.

Jude does not play around with words in an attempt to softsoap them. He is not being vindictive. He is only telling the truth, the whole truth, and nothing but the truth. God is against them!

The Greek word *'ouai'* speaks of a culmination of calamity and pathos, of hopelessness and sorrow. It is an emphatic denunciation. Their destiny is ominous. The future for these religious cranks is foreboding. And, to make matters worse, there is no prospect of recovery. They have overstepped the mark. They have gone beyond the point of no return.

Once this act of spiritual treachery takes place and the sentence has been announced it is irrevocable and final. No plea of mitigating circumstances will be heard. They have brought it on themselves. They have noone else to blame.

To skim across the surface of the verse it would appear that Jude is picking a few individuals out of the hat. But these men were not chosen at random. They were selected by the Spirit because of their eminent suitability.

Individually, they speak of one aspect of what it means to fall away from the truth; when taken together they present a more complete picture and image.

There is nothing static in the text. There is no hint of a halt or a turning back. No U-turn is anticipated. It is recklessly hurtling down the slippery slope to hell.

It is a vicious circle and should serve as a terse warning to those on the fringe of the fellowship. Apostates first enter upon a wrong path, they then run rapidly down that road, finally they perish at the end of it. They are like a runaway car careering dangerously down a steep gradient. To change the metaphor, what began in a small way has snowballed out of control.

They tampered with the truth. Then they twisted the truth. And, sadly, they then turned away from the truth. This is the life and death of a synthetic saint.

Jude points the finger and declares they have *'taken the*

way of Cain.' They are guilty of rationalism. He thinks his way is better and more acceptable than God's. He felt grieved and dejected when God rejected his offering and accepted his brother Abel's. Actually, the major difference was the blood!

Cain set aside the blood of sacrifice and thought he could still gain access into God's presence. He believed God would be satisfied with the agricultural produce of his hands. But He wasn't. He wanted to do his own thing and go his own way. He sought to get the upper hand and play a game of one-upmanship in his attitude towards God.

Other fervent impostors have *'rushed for profit into Balaam's error.'* That means they have put a price on their ministry. Money is the bottom line. If the price is right they would do anything or go anywhere. They were preaching for what they could get out of it. A fat cheque at the end of a service. Not faith but a fee! It is the *'loadsamoney'* mentality.

They were guilty of compromise as they straddled the fence. They tried to run with the foxes and hunt with the hounds - a sheer impossibility. They knowingly sacrificed eternal riches for temporal benefits. They exercised a compelling desire to acquire some part of the world even at the expense of losing their own soul. They were in the dock for milking believers dry for hard cash and *'dollar currency'*. They stifled their own convictions for short-lived gain.

Apostates are likened to the rebellion of Korah which is recorded in Numbers 16. He planned an insurrection against the leaders of Israel. It was anarchy. Along with some colleagues he hatched a plot to overthrow the Lord's servant. Their ulterior motive was fired by jealousy.

But God had the last laugh. The ground opened up in a moment and they perished. The earth swallowed them. God had vindicated his servants. And he always does!

Cain ignored the word, Balaam opposed the word, but Korah rebelled against the word of God. He thought he and his so-called friends were doing the nation a favour. In reality, they were standing against the mind and purpose of

God. And they paid the price. They contravened God's law. Therefore, they carried the can!

The alarming tendency today is to fragment and break up into all shapes and sizes of groups scattered here and there and yonder. Little meetings filled with discontented church members soon become the ideal breeding ground for party political activists to wave their distinctive banner. Splits are happening virtually every week as men gather a few around them and begin to build their own empire. It is well nigh impossible to monitor the situation as it is changing almost daily. It becomes a veritable hotch-potch as so many are jumping on the bandwagon.

God is not amused. Neither is he impressed. Those who dearly love the Lord must endeavour to keep the unity of the Spirit in such a manner that befits the gospel of Christ.

These three illustrations are pertinent. They have succeeded in showing us that, even though there may be new faces, their errors are as old as the hills.

Selah ...
Whether we are walking with God or engaged in worship of God there is only one way of approach: the precious blood.

13

FIVE TALKING PICTURES

"These men are blemishes at your love feasts, eating with you without the slightest qualm - shepherds who feed only themselves. They are clouds without rain, blown along by the wind; autumn trees, without fruit and uprooted - twice dead. They are wild waves of the sea, foaming up their shame; wandering stars, for whom blackest darkness has been reserved for ever" (verses 12,13)

The Bible reveals to us that those whose faith and fellowship is merely synthetic are easily detected. Jude deploys five metaphors or similes in a valiant attempt to show these infiltrators in their true colours. He unmasks them.

The penman, in his extensive use of illustration, has already covered the whole of creation, from angels to men to animals. Nature is the missing link. Here, in two verses, he makes amends as he brings before us the earth, the air, the trees, the sea, and the starry heavens. These are windows from the world of nature.

I'm sure this fiery outburst from Jude must have rocked the very foundations of the local assembly. He goes at them with all guns blazing. How does he describe them?

They are, firstly, *'blemishes in your love feasts.'* Another translation depicts them as *'hidden rocks.'* An apostate is, therefore, like the tip of an iceberg. Very little of his spurious activity may be visible initially but sooner rather than later there will be a disaster of titanic proportions. Their danger is unseen. But the point of impact is of serious consequence. Shipwrecked saints!

These pretenders were participating at the weekly love feast which was an ideal occasion for sweet fellowship around a common meal. It was shared by all in the congregation and was the highlight of the day as they demonstrated openly their love for the Lord in a practical way towards each other.

It was the prelude to the Breaking of Bread as reflected in 1 Corinthians 11. These people were making a travesty of the agape lunch. They greedily indulged their appetites to the full. They fared sumptuously and had no qualms or reservations of conscience about their unrestrained activities. They had no hang-ups as they were thinking only of themselves.

They threatened the stability and buoyancy of the whole company. They were in danger of going under. The peril of running aground was blatantly obvious as time wore on. The false teacher surrounded his error with reams of verbal junk and a sprinkling of pseudopiety. All the time the jagged reef of his doctrinal unreliability was crouching below the surface.

The tragedy of the early church was that genuine believers in many cases did not recognise these spiritual masqueraders until it was too late. How many fellowships today, sailing on the ocean of love and harmony, have run aground on synthetic saints who, like hidden rocks, have brought in their wake division, dissension and disunity.

Secondly, he views them as *'clouds without rain.'* What a potent picture that is especially to the eastern mind. Very often farmers and agricultural employees would scan the sky at certain seasons for the appearance of a cloud. When that fleecy cumulus did appear, they rejoiced at the promise of rain. Nothing could be more unreal and eventually more disappointing than a waterless cloud. This was the exact representation of these false teachers: synthetic saints.

The appearance is hopeful but the goods are not delivered.

They were fraudulent. False promises. Their productivity was non-existent. It was nil!

We need to remember that Jude was writing to second generation believers. It was maybe forty years or so after the day of Pentecost. Those were days of revival drought. Christianity was born in revival. Thousands upon thousands had been swept into the kingdom of God on a tide of unprecedented blessing. The power of God was unleashed. The whole world was aware of what was happening. But, in the second generation, these phenomena had largely disappeared.

In between times, these emissaries of hell came along and infiltrated their fellowship causing mega-chaos. They assured the people they had the answer to the prevailing problems. They offered new ideas, bigger and better ways of tackling the thorny issues, they promised a spiritual breakthrough if they pursued a certain course of action. But, Jude candidly says, they were clouds without water. All talk and no action.

They are blown along with the wind. They are fad followers. They leap on the latest gravy train. They want to investigate everything that is new and conduct a review of anything that is in vogue. Jude's considered estimation of them is that they are shallow and stupid. We ought to be able to see through them. With all their expertise and professional attempts at public relations they failed to give much needed refreshment. They were as dry as dust.

Jude, in his third sketch, portrays them as *'autumn trees'* that are *'without fruit and uprooted.'* Here he is saying much the same as before only employing a different simile. There is appearance but no substance. Fruit is conspicuous by its absence. There is barrenness and sterility. They are void of any precious life giving sap.

They have been uprooted because they are useless. The fire was the best and only place for them. That, sadly, is the fate of these artificial believers who lack authenticity. They are not joined to the Vine and so they will never bloom or blossom in spring. They are dead through and through.

There is nothing viable that can be done with then - they are beyond repair or renewal. They are dead. As if to emphasise their utter lostness Jude says they are *'twice dead'*. It was the beloved evangelist D. L. Moody who is reputed to have said, "Where a man is born once, he will have to die twice; but where a man is born twice, he will have to die but once."

Fourthly, in his penultimate analogy, he says they are like *'wild waves of the sea.'* It was the prophet Isaiah who described the godless as being like the troubled sea. It is never at rest. Its foaming waves incessantly beat upon the shore depositing the flotsam and jetsam which defile the ocean. The beaches are always littered with unsightly and unseemly objects when the frothing spray and spume has subsided. The aftermath is one of filth.

So it is with the apostate. Given time his real character will be revealed. When the storms of life come and the chilling winds of adversity beat upon his heart then the real man emerges. Generally, it is not a pleasant sight. What is lying fermenting on the ocean bed of his innermost being is thrown up in public for all to see. He has exposed himself for what he really is. His life is one worthy of a refuse tip. It is rubbish.

And, finally, Jude moves higher to the heavens as he sets before us another snapshot of these erstwhile pretenders to the throne. They are *'wandering stars.'*

Our present world is one of a family of planets revolving around the sun, lighted by the sun, and controlled by the sun. Sometimes a wandering body from outer space is seen entering the atmosphere, flashing brilliantly for a moment, then either dashing onward in its erratic course into outer space again, or becoming a dark cinder through friction with the air. Shooting stars are a picture of synthetic saints.

They have no sense of direction and lack a clear sense of purpose in life. They flicker briefly then their light is extinguished. They come and they go. Here one day and gone the next.

These exuberant gentlemen with an overdose of charisma often parade themselves in our day. We admire and are bowled over by their brilliance and are often dazzled by their long list of qualifications and apparently excellent credentials. These spiritual salesmen are trafficking in divine goods as they offer the latest gimmicks and gadgets to unsuspecting and sometimes gullible christian consumers.

These apostates are living their lives out of orbit. Often times they are a flash in the pan. In reality, at the end of the journey, they are destined for the *'blackness of darkness.'* What an end. Where light never penetrates they will wander for eternity.

Selah ...

Take a second look at these five pictures and compare the synthetic saint with the real believer in the here and now and in the there and then. On which side of the fence are you sitting?

14

A ROSE IN THE MIDST OF THORNS

"Enoch, the seventh from Adam, prophesied about these men" (verse 14a)

You may be surprised to find Enoch's name mentioned in the book of Jude. It seems oddly out of place. He is like a rose in the midst of thorns. But, it is only in the midst of such blackness that the translucent light of his character shines forth. He is a beacon not a falling star!

Enoch is the epitome of godliness. He is the ideal model to emulate if we are to know anything of a life of walking with God. There is hardly another bible character who vies with him in challenging us to a deeper devotional life. Yet, the amazing thing is that in the pages of scripture he is rarely mentioned. All his remarkable achievements under God are compressed and compacted neatly into a sparse handful of verses. You can almost count them on ten fingers!

He was not the founding father of a nation life Abraham, nor a charismatic leader like Moses, nor a conquering warrior like Gideon, nor an eminent statesman like Daniel.

From reading between the lines it appears that he was a common five-eight whose heart God had touched. He was a countryman whose life the Lord had graciously transformed. Yet, alongside Noah, he shares the distinction of being a man of whom it was said *'he walked with God.'*

He is identified in verse 14 as being *'the seventh from Adam.'* The reason why is obvious. He was of the godly line from Adam and not from the secondary line of Cain as in Genesis 4:17. He is a different branch in the family tree!

His name means *'dedicated.'* And he lived up to his name. He is a remarkable example of a God-centred and God-controlled life.

Life for him was far from easy. He lived and worked in dark and difficult times. He was part of the antedeluvian civilisation which bore the marks and felt the repercussions of Adam's sin. It was an age when sin abounded and moral principles were deliberately swept aside. The caption over his era is found in Genesis 6:5 where we read concerning man that *'every inclination of the thoughts of his heart was only evil all the time.'* Times were bad!

However, in the midst of such evil and reprobate behaviour, he continued to walk with God and he bore a silent testimony to Jehovah.

God blessed him when, at the age of 65, he was presented with a son by his wife. It was his firstborn. Selecting a name was no problem. God had given him a revelation that, when this child should die, every living creature upon the earth would be destroyed by a universal flocd. That's why he called him *'Methuselah'*, meaning, *'when he is dead it shall be sent.'*

Something happened at this juncture in Enoch's life. He came into a closer and more meaningful relationship with the Lord. And, for three centuries after he walked with God on the highway of life.

It must have been extremely tough at times. He was probably ostracised by those in the community as they reckoned he was some kind of oddball-cum-religious fanatic. He was the butt of much ridicule and no doubt mean individuals would have made him the lead character in their smutty smear stories. His was a lonely path.

He was able to keep going because God was with him. That made all the difference. And, one day his confidence and trust in God was amply rewarded. He was ushered into the immediate presence of God without experiencing death. He escaped it. The grave was not his goal. The patriarchal funeral bell tolled ominously in Genesis 5 many times. But not for him. He was different. He left this world not by the dark tunnel of death but by the golden bridge of translation.

His was a royal entrance into the eternal home of God. For Enoch, it was merely a change of location not a change of company. Faith gave way to sight and promise became reality.

But he left behind him a clear-cut testimony in that *'he pleased God.'* That's dedication with a capital 'D'. He was a spiritual giant among his pygmy contemporaries and it was only when he was gone that they realised and readily acknowledged his enormous influence for good in their midst. Yes, a rose among thorns!

Selah ...

It's so easy to play the christian life as though it were a game of trivial pursuits. We make all sorts of lame-duck excuses as to why we are the way we are. God has not changed. He is looking for others to follow in the footsteps of Enoch and enjoy a life of walking with Himself. Are you being singled out in the crowd? Perhaps!

15

CHRIST IS COMING ...

"See, the Lord is coming with thousands upon thousands of his holy ones to judge everyone, and to convict all the ungodly of all the ungodly acts they have done in the ungodly way, and of all the harsh words ungodly sinners have spoken against him" (verses 14b,15)

It's hard to believe, but Enoch was a prophet before the Flood. His was a two pronged double-barrelled message. Jesus is coming. And, judgement is coming. With such a twin thrust he did not mince his words. He didn't need to because he knew God would sort everything and everyone out in His own time. That is what Jude believed. Hence, his open letter to the churches.

His first word, *'see'*, is an attempt by him to get others to listen carefully as something important is about to follow. He pleads for their undivided attention as he divulges a vital piece of information to them.

He heralded forth with clarity and earnest conviction the message of the second advent of Jesus Christ. He preached enthusiastically about the coming of the Lord! Is it any wonder he said *'see.'* This is the backbone of his message.

It adds a new dimension to it. It gives him fresh impetus as he attacks these shameless synthetic saints. With this great assurance burning in his soul he fearlessly denounced and forthrightly condemned these ambassadors of Satan.

Their foolish activities were both subversive and perversive. Jude was resolute and unflinching in his stand for purity of fellowship and doctrine because he knew Christ was returning. But he doesn't stop there. He proceeds to show the reason why He is coming and with whom He is coming.

When the signal is given for him to break through the clouds he will not be alone. Rather, he will be accompanied in regal splendour with *'thousands upon thousands of his holy ones.'* Oh yes, the angels will be at his side but so too will his believing people. We comprise the entourage that is referred to in Revelation 19 as the *'armies of heaven'*. It will be a scene of magnificence and majesty as the King returns to planet earth.

This has all to do with the bringing to fruition of the blessed hope of the people of God. One day the heavens will glow with splendour and every eye will be fixed on the sky. All over the world men will behold the undiluted and unrivalled wonder of the King of Kings returning. In that day he will be admired and glorified in his saints and hardened sinners will recognise and confess that Jesus is Lord. So too will the synthetic saints! It is to deal with them and their companions that He has come.

After his feet touch down on the Mount of Olives he will swiftly inaugurate his policy of firm and fair retribution and justice will be seen to be done. He is coming as Judge and in that capacity He will pass sentence on those who have withstood his gracious overtures. Right will triumph over wrong. Error will be vanquished by truth.

In verse 15 there is one word which is repeated four times. It is the word *'ungodly.'* That's what Jude thinks of these apostates. They have left God out of their calculations. They are bereft of any sense of awe and reverence towards Him. Their lives are destitute as they lived a lie. In the final analysis, they only fooled themselves.

The *'harsh words these ungodly sinners have spoken against him'* is an expression that is indicative of all the blasphemous propaganda that flowed from their lips with apparent fluency and relative ease. They became victims of their own verbosity.

Sinners in the dock. At the bar of God their sensuous deeds testified against them. Their works and impropriety spoke out against them as they froze on the spot. They had been caught on. They can't pull the wool over his eyes nor can they hide from his all-seeing eye.

They had talked themselves into it. Now they can't talk their way out of it. It's too late. Then, the tables will have turned. The ball will be fairly and squarely in their court. They will be on the receiving end. They have no defense. They have no leg to stand on. They have no right of appeal. Their destiny is settled.

Selah ...

Sometimes when we look around us and see what is happening we say with the Psalmist: 'How long, O Lord?' But, Christ will come and cause His enemies to be his footstool. We tend to forget that the last chapter has not yet been written in the book of their lives. God has not forgotten!

75

16

VICTIMS OF VIOLENCE

*" These men are grumblers and fault-finders; they follow
their own evil desires; they boast about themselves and
flatter others for their own advantage" (verse 16)*

Jude has made it plain in the course of his comments that
lawlessness is the hallmark of these synthetic saints. Violence raises its ugly head in their pursuit of some kind of
religious experience. Godlessness, as we saw in the previous
chapter, is a by-product of such a fiendish philosophy.

This weird evil stems from the fact that they have no
respect for God or any form of structured human authority.
They are guilty of spiritual terrorism. They are engaged in
guerilla warfare in the local church. They are the godfathers
of religious violence.

These diehards are *'grumblers.'* That's an easily recognis-
able trait in their crooked character. (Incidentally, this is the
only time this particular word appears in the New Testament). It means someone who harps on about something and
doesn't know when to keep quiet. It typifies the person who
has a bee on their bonnet and who will not rest until they have
aired their point of view. He is thinking about those who
discontentedly complain.

In the original language it carried the idea of the cooing of
doves! Well, these infidels were certainly not bird-mouthed!

It is not a loud outspoken dissatisfaction. It is a constant
undercurrent of incessant muttering below the breath. The

person may not be clearly heard or readily understood but they have succeeded in registering a protest. Verbal rumbling. This attitude betrays a spirit of acrimony.

Their murmuring involved three basic denials. These ingredients are all found in the modern day apostate as they were evident in Jude's day. These people deplore the providence of God, they despise the provision of God, and they denounce the person of God.

However, Jude goes a step further. Not only do they murmur and grumble but they also *'find fault.'* They had the unenviable knack of complaining and saying the wrong thing at the right time. One always leads to the other.

Nothing was ever right. They were a miserable bunch. They were unhappy with their lot in life and they projected their pent up feelings on those in the congregation. Nothing ever measured up to their high standards. They were always poking holes and finding fault. Theirs was a ministry of pulling down rather than building up. No matter what it was it proved to be a perennial bone of contention.

They seemed to have the perpetual habit of falling out of the wrong side of the bed.

These men were the liberal theologians of the early church. They were the modernists of Jude's day. They wanted to adopt a different approach to the word of God and advised others to give more credence to the traditions of men. Relentlessly they waged a battle against all and sundry as they gradually undermined the very foundation of not a few.

Buttonholed and cajoled many gave in. Anything for a quiet life was the mentality of so many. It was easier to go with the crowd than it was to stand up and be counted against these fault-finders. They are malicious men and their tactics are disturbing as they fleece the flock. They are always right! Everyone else is wrong. Their way is the only way.

The third numbing characteristic of these apostates is their inkling to *'follow their own evil desires.'* They were slaves to their sin. It is not only a lust for sexual gratification but it can also refer to the passionate craving for some other object of good or evil intent. By and large their activity was geared not to the spiritual part of man's makeup but to his carnal and fleshly appetite.

They were not acting on impulse. Neither were they acting on the spur of the moment. Nor were they perpetrating their acts of pointless violence only when a tingling feeling was felt at the base of their spine.

Their behaviour was planned and premeditated. Their strategy was mapped out and their goals clearly defined. Their outlook was libertine. Their policy was hedged in anti-nomian phraseology. They were freedom fighters and in their own eyes the end justified the means.

Deluded they were. They were drunk with a feeling of their self importance. They spent their time *'boasting about themselves.'* They were loud mouthed and big mouthed. They were famed for their notoriety. They were double talkers both in private and in public. Whether in a room or at the rostrum they would soon win an argument and woo another unsuspecting individual. They were devious. They showed utter contempt as they attacked the mind and intelligence of others around them.

They were conceited and acted in a high-handed manner. They were audacious and pompous in their dealings with ordinary people. They could not be pinned down on any aspect of truth because of their profoundly arrogant style and their ability to side-step and dodge controversy.

Sometimes they were like a babbling brook. Other times they were like a river bursting its banks.

To listen to them the average person would be mesmerised and held spellbound. One could be forgiven for thinking they had swallowed the dictionary the evening before. Yet, when their speeches came under the close scrutiny of the literary critics they were found to be empty and nothing more than fizz and foam. From beginning to end it was froth and bubble.

They were among the foundation members of the mutual

admiration society. Membership of this exclusive club depended on one's ability to brag about one's own comprehensive achievements whether real or imagined. This was right down their street as they were the best flatterers in the district. They flattered themselves and enlarged their personal ego. They flattered others but always diverted the attention back to themselves. They loved the limelight.

The final distinguishing trademark of these merchandisers of error is recorded by Jude as being their inherent ability to steal the show by *'flattering others for their own advantage.'* Their outlook in life revolved around me, myself and I. They were self-centred as they continually looked after *'number one.'* They were intoxicated with their own personality cult.

Because of their inner confidence in their inate ability and their inflated awareness that they couldn't be done without they were able to manipulate men and coerce others into their line of thinking. They created situations for their personal gain and benefit and with the passing of days many people were eating out of their hands.

They had been given a foothold and it was not long until they established themselves at the control panel. They were innocently given an inch and they took a mile.

That may alarm us. But, that is the way apostates work!

Selah ...
We have been forewarned. Now, thanks to Jude, we are forearmed!

17

APOSTOLIC PROPHETS

"But, dear friends, remember what the apostles of our Lord Jesus Christ foretold, They said to you, 'in the last times there will be scoffers who will follow their own ungodly desires'" (verses 17,18)

Yes, the apostles in the first century had a message foretelling what was going to happen. It was a prophetic utterance. Their prediction came true!

It has been heavy going so far in Jude's little letter. At times it has felt as though we have been walking through a long dark tunnel. The horizon seemed to be slowly receding into the distance with each verse. He left no stone unturned as he sought with every means at his disposal to highlight the very real problems within the church. It was something to wrestle with. They had to grapple with it.

Now, in verse 17, the opening word would seem to indicate that the dawn is breaking through the gloom. There is a light at the end of the proverbial tunnel. It is only one word. He says *'but.'* It signals a reversal. The church can make its presence felt. It can effectively deal with these synthetic saints.

The original conveys the idea of *'but as for you.'* The contrast between the real believers and these cosmetic christians is quite incredible. There is a vast gulf that cannot be spanned between truth and error. They are poles apart.

Again, he refers to the saints, as *'dear friends.'* He can't say that about the opposition. Certainly not! It is an open display of warmth and affection as he tries to assure them they are still very much upon his heart. His opinion of them is unchanged even though they have been dragged through a hedge backwards.

Perhaps they were tempted to think that Jude was alone in his thinking and appraisal of their situation. They maybe thought he was over reacting to the present climate in their christian fellowships. Rightly or wrongly they may have assumed he was swinging the pendulum to the opposite extreme. But, to be fair, he wasn't.

Their spiritual forefathers had said this would happen. Their one time contemporaries had warned of something similar. The way forward for them was not to adopt some new innovation but to rediscover what had been previously revealed. They were called upon to remember.

But what? Well, the words of the other apostles. Namely, Paul and Peter. They both mentioned it. For example, Paul in Acts 20:29; 1 Timothy 4:1; and 2 Timothy 3 talked about it. His message is self contained and self explanatory. Peter, likewise, in his second epistle says much the same (cf. 2 Peter 3). Jude was hoping they would be able to recall these quotations and a host of others.

They could not afford to neglect these pertinent warnings. It was do or die! If they did, the consequences would be serious and catastrophic in that the local testimony would become a centre for false religion and the light would be extinguished. The apostles hit the nail on the head and if the early church failed to listen they would take a hammering from the devil in the guise of these synthetic saints.

What is causing Jude more heartache than anything else is that this situation need not have arisen in the first place. They had been well warned. The danger lights were flashing red. This round of trouble could have been averted and avoided if only they had listened and paid rapt attention to the servants of the Lord. Their boat was being rocked with the tidal wave of erroneous doctrine and a lot of shilly-shallying in matters of faith and practice.

Jude proceeds to reinforce his argument by reminding them of the apostles warning and description of these tyrants in their midst. He calls them scoffers. The Greek word implies *'to act in a childish fashion, to be childish, to play and to jest.'* And, didn't they excel!

They lack maturity. They are overgrown babies always wanting to be mollycoddled. These are the people who know not when and where to draw the line. They habitually go over the top. They are always jesting and have the despicable trait of making light of everything no matter how serious it is. Life is treated as one big joke.

They lived and worked as if they were answerable to nobody. They were responsible alone for their irresponsible actions. In reality, no-one could work with them.

The most protruding feature in their personality is that *'they follow their own ungodly desires.'* It sticks out a mile. They are prisoners to their own perversity and are in bondage to their own badness. They are fettered to their own flesh. They are endlessly campaigning for civil rights in the local fellowship and in the process sowing seeds of discontent and strife. And they succeeded. Otherwise, Jude would not have written what he did.

They would worm their way into churches in the last times. This means that even though the words of Jude were directed to meet a very specific need in the first century church they still have a strikingly real application to the church down through the ages. And, never more so, than today.

Selah ...
Our eyes have been opened to the great need in our generation. Are our ears open to hear the word of God telling us what to do? They are living in a vacuum in a world of their own making. They need to see reality in our profession of faith.

83

18

SPLITTING A CHURCH

*"These are the men who divide you, who follow mere
natural instincts and do not have the Spirit" (verse 19)*

Jude is now tying up the loose ends in his argument against
these false teachers posing as synthetic saints. His conclu-
sion is short and straight to the point. He labels them for what
they are. He tells it like it is. There are three things worth
noting.

Firstly, they are church splitters. They cause division and
discord. They make factions in the fellowship. They disrupt
the life of the local assembly and bring disunity among the
members. They are troublemakers.

They spread rumour and gossip about the leaders in the
local church which ultimately brings about their downfall.
The apostates were hailed as the saviours of the situation.
Some of the members supported those who had been ousted
whilst others gave their backing to those who had wormed
their way to the top via the rear door. These individuals felt
they were among the spiritual elite. They were guilty of
exclusivism. They drew a circle to shut men out instead of
drawing a circle to take men in.

Secondly, they are set before us as those *'who follow mere
natural instincts.'* We have this thought brought out earlier
in the epistle as Jude reminds us forcefully of their selfseek-
ing ambition. They will polarise the church community by
adopting a sectarian spirit. In following their natural instincts

there is nothing spiritual about them. They are, rather, soulish. That is the domineering trend in their attitude and the governing factor in their actions. They were earth bound in their reasoning. They are worldly minded.

And, thirdly, Jude reminds us that *'they have not the Spirit.'* They were devoid of the Spirit of God in their lives. He was not alive in their hearts. They knew nothing of the power of God in their lives. They had never experienced anything of the ministry of the Spirit within them or upon them. He was completely foreign to them.

This is the decisive note in Jude's description and it clinches the argument. Because the Spirit is not in residence in their lives it means they are not part of the family of God. Jude makes it abundantly clear that they are not even christians. They are still sinners.

If there were any remaining questions lurking in the back of our mind as to whether an apostate is a lost soul or merely a christian who is mistaken in some of his ideas, this certainly settles it. He is an unregenerate person. He lacks the distinguishing mark of the true believer. The divine imprimatur is not graven on his heart.

Selah ...

These self-styled spiritual masqueraders were the religious bourgeoisis of the day. But that did not deter Jude from saying what he did. Why should it?

19

BE WHAT YOU ARE

"But you, dear friends" (verse 20a)

They were saints! Not the kind you see in chapels and cathedrals emblazoned in stained glass windows. No! They were never canonised. But, they had been cleansed from sin.

Undoubtedly, some of those in the local assembly were wondering where they stood in relation to God after such a blistering attack from Jude on these impostors. Perhaps they felt unsure and uncertain. Again, Jude reminds them that they are *'dear friends.'*

They are just as much a saint as he is!

Sometimes we think a saint is a particularly good christian who really loves the Lord more than we do. We may set them on a pedestal and view them as a kind of honours graduate in christian living. That's an unfortunate digression from the biblical concept.

We are saints and *'dear friends'* because we have been brought into a vital and vibrant relationship with the Lord. We are saints even though we are very much alive and well on this earth. We still have a job to do for Jesus. We have been chosen by the Lord and indwelt by the Spirit. We have been brought to this position in spite of our past history of bad works. As saints we are different. And, we are meant to be.

As christians they belonged to each other because they first belonged to the Lord. Jude is reassuring them: you really are dear friends.

At times they may not feel like it ... but they are. At times they may not look like it ... but they are. At times they may not act like it ... but they are. It's a fact that can't be stressed enough. No one can ride slipshod over them. They belong to God.

The indisputable fact remains that alongside them we are all members of the church of Jesus Christ of present day saints!

Selah ...

You can say to yourself today if you know the Lord Jesus: 'I am a saint.' There is nothing arrogant or bombastic about that. It is a statement of fact. You are. Now, go out and be one ...

20

A PACKAGE FOR SURVIVAL

" ... build yourselves up in your most holy faith and pray in the Holy Spirit. Keep yourselves in God's love as you wait for the mercy of our Lord Jesus Christ to bring you to eternal life" (verses 20,21)

If they wanted to keep their heads above water this was what Jude wisely encouraged them to do. This syllabus would enable them to survive in the midst of such debilitating and trying circumstances. When others were going down and under they would be able to walk tall with their faith rooted and fixed in God.

This was the way forward. There were no short cuts. There was no easy road to success. It would involve sheer hard graft and consolidated effort on their part but at the end of the day it would prove to be eminently worthwhile.

There will obviously be short-term advantages by avidly pursuing such a curriculum. But, the maximum benefit to be gleaned from following such a course will only be derived in the long-term. Jude is not thinking about today or even tomorrow. It is the day after which is uppermost in his mind.

There are four facets to this ongoing programme in our survival package. They should be taken together as a corporate entity and not hatched off singly or separately. They are intertwined and interlinked. One will automatically lead to the other thereby ensuring continuity and a measure of consistency in our spiritual growth and development. We will, therefore, not become lopsided in our striving after maturity. We will become *'all round'* believers.

He exhorts us, initially, to *'build yourselves up in your most holy faith.'* Here is practical theology at its finest and best. Here is the christian dressed in his dungarees. He puts on his working clothes. This is a do-it-yourself study module. It is a piece of sound and sensible advice imploring us to get our act together.

Jude is not thinking here of their personal faith in Jesus Christ as Saviour and Lord. Rather, he is reverting back to what he spoke of earlier in his letter, when he mentioned *'the Faith once entrusted to the saints.'* It is the written word. It is the truth of God, penned by men of God, under the control and illumination of the Spirit of God, for all the people of God.

With characteristic flair he describes the faith as being *'most holy.'* Not just *'holy'* which is sufficiently adequate in itself. But he goes a step further and says *'most holy.'* It is a concept he wants to underscore so it will have an indelible impression upon them. It is something graciously imparted by God to men. It suggests the sacred nature of such a revelation. It is out of this world in that it is heavenly in origin and divine in essence.

The word of God is sure and stedfast. It proves to be an anchor for the soul of man in the many storms of life. When the sands of time are shifting and sinking we have something we can grasp and tenaciously hold on to.

Come what may, the Faith will always remain intact and unaffected by the chilling winds of liberal theology and howling storms of apostasy. The word of God stands un-moved amidst the gales of higher criticism that have been levelled against it. There is not even the slightest trace of a crack nor is there any sign of strain being imposed on the infrastructure. Today it towers o'er the many wrecks of time.

Did you notice how personal it is? He says *'your most holy faith.'* Oh yes it is God's word and in that sense it belongs to him. But when we are brought into a saving relationship with his dear Son that which is his then becomes ours as well. It becomes mine!

The word *'your'* is inextricably linked with the word *'yourselves'* in that here is something for us to do. We have a solemn responsibility to spend time with the Word, and around the Word, in private as well as in our regular attendance at the house of God. What we hear from other gifted expositors should only supplement our own diet.

From observation it seems to me that it is much easier to be a spiritual sponge than it is to be a serious student of the word. How many there are who prefer to soak everything up that they hear from the pulpit and neglect their personal quiet time. The majority prefer to be spoonfed and treated as babes in a nursery environment instead of making the earnest effort and getting into it ourselves.

Jude is talking about building. And, it is in the present tense which implies it is an ongoing occupation. This is a fulltime activity year in year out. The more we put into it the more we will get out of it.

It will mean hard work. It will take determination and dedication. It will involve discipline. The milk and meat of the word are provided so that we might progress down the road to maturity in Christ. We will develop spiritual muscle but we need to keep in shape. We need to tone up daily as we diligently exercise our mind and heart before an open book. Faith and flab are not compatible.

The second guideline Jude gives is to *'pray in the Holy Spirit.'* When we read the word God is communicating with us. As we engage in prayer we are communing with God. It is God speaking to us then we respond by talking with Him.

Prayer is something we talk so much about but rarely do. We know more about it in our minds than we may have experienced in our hearts.

Prayer is not a shopping list. It is not rushing in and out of the presence of God with a list of requests. It is taking time to linger and wait in his presence and simply adoring and worshipping him. That is what he longs for and desires that we might do.

The prayer that wins the Father's approval is the one prayed in the Holy Ghost. This is the prayer that delights the father's heart and one which he takes pleasure in answering. This is the prayer that brings a welcome response from the throne.

To *'pray in the Holy Spirit'* means that we must really begin to appreciate some of the wonder surrounding His name. He is the Holy Spirit. He is someone with a real and distinctive personality. At the same time, he is divine. He is God.

Before we even begin to pray we should stop for a moment to understand his ministry in our hearts and lives. It is only when we see who he is and what he is that we will be inclined to give him his rightful place in our lives. Then, perhaps, we will thank God for the gift of his Spirit.

The fact that we do pray seems to suggest that we have a need in our lives. Otherwise, why bother? It means we need God to step into a situation and intervene. We have concluded that He alone can provide the answers to our problems and the only one who can undo the tangle we find ourselves in.

We may not feel like praying but that is the time to do it. The longer we delay the more used we will become to living our lives without him. We will eventually become conditioned to such a cool relationship that we will spiritually begin to shiver and ultimately our salvation will became a frozen asset.

The way to prevent spiritual suffocation as we inhale the polluted atmosphere of the world is to linger in the presence of Jesus and breathe in the fresh air of heaven. If we don't, we will find ourselves overcome with the fumes which will cause spiritual asphyxiation.

God is waiting on the end of the line for us to call Him. The way is opened up because of Calvary. The lines are open now!

To *'pray in the Holy Spirit'* means we are totally yielded to the Spirit. We are surrounded by Him daily and know his presence and power but we should be surrendered to Him.

This is praying in the will of God. This is the prayer that never fails or falters. There is always an answer in the affirmative. He is the one who likes to say *'yes!'* And, he is the one who is listening intently to our every sigh. He is willing to aid us and help us in our many moments of crisis and need. That is what he is there for and that is why he is only a prayer away.

The third factor in Jude's four pronged manifesto is to *'keep yourselves in God's love.'* This is a burden placed fairly and squarely on our shoulders. We have to keep ourselves. The onus is on us. No one else can do it for us. We cannot share it or shelve it.

This is an exercise we need to constantly work at and daily work out. If we falter here we will have reached our spiritual Waterloo.

This is a daunting task and may appear to be a tough assignment. We will need to mobilise all our resources within if we are to stay in such a wonderful position of being in the love of God.

The best illustration of this concept is found in the parable of Luke 15. It is the familiar story of the prodigal son. Here was a young lad who turned his back on home and all that it stood for. He took his money and went on an expedition into another land. He crossed the border and began to live it up. He spent his money on wine, women and song. It wasn't long until he was penniless and hungry. He didn't have two pennies to rub together. The jingle had gone from his pockets. There's only holes there now. Life was just one big horrible mess. He ended up living in a pigsty feasting on pigswill.

But, you know, all the time the boy was away from home

the father never changed in his attitude towards him. He was still his son and he dearly loved him. However, the son removed himself from the place where he could enjoy to the full the benefits of the father's love. He wasn't in the place where his father could bless him.

He was the loser. He gained nothing from flirting with the world and having a mad spending spree. He could look back in later years and put it all down to *'experience.'* But, he really missed out. Now, that he has gone back, he appreciates his father's love more than he did before.

To be in the sphere and environment of the Father's love is to be what he wants us to be and to be where he wants us to be.

Number four would lead us to consider what it means to *'wait for the mercy of our Lord Jesus Christ to bring us to eternal life.'*

This is a forward look into the future. This is living our lives in the future tense. It is something exciting as we face the prospect that it can only get better. We are born for glory, we are bound for glory and one day we will be in the glory. This is all attributed exclusively to the mercy of our God.

It is something we should readily anticipate as if it may happen today. It could! Jesus is coming. He is returning to take us home to heaven. What a day that promises to be. Then, the eternal life we enjoy now, will be fully realised as we walk around his home and enjoy his company for ever.

His advent is imminent and impending. When we read the signs of the times and are aware that apostasy is one of them we become increasingly convinced that we can't be around here too much longer. The best is yet to be.

We will want to be ready to meet him as he breaks through the clouds. Anticipating the sound of the trumpet we will be sitting on the edge of our seats. We will be standing on our tiptoes. We will be up and about keenly awaiting the moment of callup. The countdown is getting lower every day. It will soon be zero hour. Then we will be with him. That will be the icing on the cake for the real believer.

The synthetic saints will be left behind to face the judgement of God. Their prospects are doom and gloom.

The future of the christian, however, is bright and beaming. It is something to get excited about. We should be jumping for joy with a lightness in our step. This good news is designed to put the sparkle back into drab and dreary lives.

Selah ...
Building speaks of working with our minds;
Praying talks of waiting upon our knees;
Keeping denotes a warming of our hearts;
Looking challenges us to watch with our eyes!

21

REACHING THE LOST

"Be merciful to those who doubt; snatch others from the fire and save them; to others show mercy, mixed with fear - hating even the clothing stained by corrupted flesh" (verses 22,23)

Real believers are not meant to live a cocooned existence and keep the message to themselves. We have a solemn obligation to share it with those around us. We should not seek to isolate ourselves from the world or even insulate ourselves from the comings and goings of modern society but we should endeavour at all costs to win the sinner to Jesus.

Jude is talking here about evangelism. Reaching out to the lost is his burden. We know the truth, therefore, we should tell it. We have the good news. The best news for a bad world. We owe it to those around us to pass it on in all its fulness.

Yes, if we are living in the word of God, in the place where God answers prayer, in the security of his heart of love, and in the hope of his soon appearing - then, we will be out on the streets winning the lost to Jesus.

These truths do not stand alone. They are an integral part of the great commission concerning our personal witness.

Jude is speaking principally of three groups of people. He speaks of those whom he categorises as sincere doubters. He refers to those who are living on the very edge of hell itself. And, he talks of those who are deeply contaminated by sin.

Each of these require different tactics if we are to win them with the gospel. We must know what bait to put on the fishing line if they are to bite.

The first batch we are to handle with mercy and compassion. These are apostates who are sincere doubters. They are unsure and uncertain as to what is happening to them and as to where they are going .

You will remember Peter's experience of walking on the water. He started out well exuding confidence but then he began to doubt. Then, he started to sink. Many today are like him as they are overcome and overwhelmed with a degree of fear.

To all such we extend a hand of tenderness, love and compassion. We can with the help of God pull them and pluck them to safety and salvation. That is what they need!

The second group classified need a totally different approach. We need courage as we seek to win them. They are living their lives on the fringes of hell. One wrong move and they're there. They're on the brink. It's as close as that.

To minister Christ to such people we need to see them as they really are. They are not beyond His grasp. They are not too far gone - He can still reach them. We need a sense of urgency. We have no time to waste or play around. We must go and get them. Delay could be fatal.

They are in grave danger of being sucked into the awful chasm of everlasting burning if we do not get there and throw out a lifeline.

To effectively reach such people we need boldness and a deep awareness of the enabling grace of God as we seek to rescue them as brands from the burning.

The third group Jude draws our attention to are those who have departed from the faith. They are apostates through and through. In seeking to reach them we must not throw caution to the wind. We must be ultra-careful in all our dealings with such individuals.

Failure to realise this could lead to us becoming ensnared with some tactical ploy of the devil. It has happened before and so many of God's servants are now on the shelf. They are spiritual castaways on a desert island. A moment of rash indiscretion can wreck a lifetime of ministry. It can happen so easily!

We must not allow ourselves to get caught in the compromise trap. Sooner rather than later a web will be woven and we will be caught in its strands. This is particularly true in dealing with members of the opposite sex. We can never be too vigilant!

There are obvious pitfalls that have repercussions both in the home and in the community. To get involved without enormous caution is sometimes to be seen to be courting spiritual disaster. Many situations today deservedly need to be handled with great care. They are fragile. We should keep our eyes wide open at all times and if it gets too hot to handle then is the time to back off and leave it prayerfully to someone else who is more competent and capable to counsel.

Yes, there were apostates in Jude's day. We have them in our generation. In spite of that, we are called to be witnesses to the saving grace of our God. We should not let them deter us or stand in our way. They need to be told as do countless others that Jesus is still in the business of saving souls.

Selah ...

Someone, somewhere is waiting for you to tell them of Jesus. Ask yourself the question: where would I be today if someone hadn't plucked up courage and told me? Then, go out and do someone a favour, and tell them.

22

THE FINAL CRESCENDO

"To him who is able to keep you from falling and to present you before his glorious presence without fault and with great joy - to the only God our Saviour be glory, majesty, power and authority, through Jesus Christ our Lord, before all ages, now and for evermore! Amen." (verses 24,25)

This is a fitting climax to Jude's letter to a group of battle weary and beleaguered believers. Their hearts are focussed on the greatness of God in the person of his beloved Son. He becomes the theme of their worship and adoration as they grow in appreciation of his attributes and intrinsic sterling qualities.

They may have felt downtrodden because these synthetic saints had virtually walked all over them. But that was not the end. There was something beyond it. There was something exceedingly better. One day it would be glory. Christianity is the only religion with a happy ending. And, that's for real!

Jude's last words are one of the finest benedictions ever pronounced and must rank alongside some of the greatest doxologies ever expressed by man. It is a paean of praise as we are lifted higher into the presence of our father.

It transcends the ordinary. It surpasses that which is

transient and superficial. It reaches into the realm of the sublime. Truly, it is magnificent. It is a celebration of the character of God.

He zooms in on the sovereignty of God in the life of the real believer. He talks about his amazing ability to do what we cannot do for ourselves. The wonderful thing is that it is not confined to the yesterdays of life nor is it reserved for all our tomorrows. Rather, it is in the present tense. He *is* able.

Oh yes He has done it before. And He can do it again. But, what matters is this, He can do it today - and now!

His power is measureless and limitless. There is nothing he cannot do. He is the God of miracles. He is the God who specialises in performing feats of incredible magnitude. He is the God of the humanly impossible.

He *'will keep us from falling.'* What a hope and what a sense of security that should plant within our breast. To know that he will keep us. That is all we need.

The apostates had fallen and made a shambles of their lives. Their lives were in an absolute mess. But, the real believer, will be kept from falling.

We can't fall from grace. That's a misnomer. We fall into it!

And so, day by day, his hand will be upon us for good. We may stumble and the old devil will trip us up. We may seem to be going fast nowhere or even round in circles but then God comes and gets us back on the right track. Yes, he will keep us. And, He will continue to keep us by his power until we reach the end of the journey. Then what will he do?

He will *'present you before his glorious presence without fault and with great joy.'* It really is quite exciting when we think of the programme God has mapped out for each of his children.

When the trumpet sounds and we are ushered into the close and near presence of Jesus we will stand before him at the judgement seat (cf. 2 Corinthians 5:10). The *'bema'* is the place of assessment for real believers. It is the hour of appraisal and our moment of examination. Then our actions will come under his scrutiny and we will see how we have fared.

After the hour of grand review has passed our Lord then presents his beautiful bride at the court of heaven. This is the thought encapsulated in the heart of Paul and often transposed in his writings to various churches in the early days (cf. 2 Corinthians 11:2; Ephesians 5:27; Colossians 1:21,22).

He will show us off to the father with enormous pleasure and satisfaction. We will be there radiant and without fault as our sin is all past and under the blood. Standing by his side we will be clad in the white linen garment of his impeccable righteousness. Perfected, we will be his pride and joy.

That is what he intends doing in the future. Jude is wanting to assure them that if he can do that at some date in the there and then he can look after them in the here and now. Surely he can!

Ascribed unto him are glory, majesty, power and authority and these serve and combine to remind us that he is omnipotent, omnipresent and omniscient. Yes, he is all-strong, he is all-seeing, and he is present in all situations. Even theirs! And yours!

What a fantastic way to end a letter! Breathtaking. Enough to blow the mind. *'Amen'* is what he says.

And, so say all of us!

Selah ...

Jude. Now you know him inside out. Thanks for listening to what he has had to say. What difference has it made in your walk with God? Is it real or synthetic?